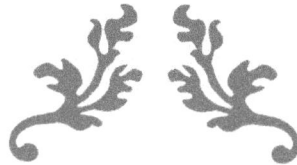

ENHANCING YOUR LEADERSHIP DNA: COACHING FOR SUCCESS

Beyond the Workshop "Workbook"

DENOLA M. BURTON
AUTHOR
CEO AND FOUNDER OF ENHANCED DNA:
DEVELOP NURTURE ACHIEVE, LLC

Enhancing Your Leadership DNA: Coaching for Success

Beyond the Workshop "Workbook"

Enhanced DNA Publishing

CONTENTS

Enhanced DNA: Develop Nurture Achieve, LLC

Enhancing Your Leadership DNA: Coaching for Success

Beyond the Workshop "Workbook"

This workbook is the follow-up to the workshop by the same name: *Enhancing Your Leadership DNA: Coaching for Success.* In the workshop, leaders were introduced to a model that allowed them to enhance their leadership (DNA) in order to be a more effective coach. They were able to practice their skills in order to improve their ability to effectively coach in any situation.

For more information about the complete workshop, please contact us at https://developnurtureachieve.com/contact.

Here is a summary of the highlights of that workshop as a review.

Summary from the Workshop

Section 1: Enhancing Your Leadership DNA:

Coaching for Success

As a result of this workshop, leaders were able to understand and improve their ability to coach for success as a result of these topics:

1. Me: As a Coach – Each participant completed a self-assessment to determine their current status as a coach. This was used to help each leader understand the key components of coaching and the gaps that they may have as a coach. Contact us if you would like to complete this assessment at https://developnurtureachieve.com/contact.
    - Conduct Self-Coaching Assessment
    - Identify gaps and areas of improvement

2. Understanding Coaching
    - What is Coaching
    - When "not" to Coach
    - Key elements of effective Coaching

3. Implementing a Coaching Model (GROW Model)
    - Goals (Using SMAART Goals)
    - Reality
    - Obstacles/Options
    - Way Forward

4. The difference between Feedback and Coaching
    - What is feedback?
        o Exercises/practice on Feedback
    - When to use feedback vs when to use coaching
        o Exercises/practice on Coaching

- Coaching through difficult conversations/conflict
  - Exercises/practice on conflict resolution (feedback and coaching)

5. How to develop/maintain a Coaching Culture
   - Created and nurtured by leaders
   - Nurturing results in transformation
   - Realizing the culture change
   - Maintaining the culture change

Practice Exercises to Reinforce Skills from the Workshop

1. Coaching Assessment: Conduct an assessment of yourself as a Coach. Use the results to identify the gaps you have and the specific areas you need to focus on to improve your coaching skills.

2. Define "Coach": Have everyone write one sentence that describes what an effective coach is. Discuss what a coach "is not" and identify examples of times that coaching is not appropriate.

3. Coaching Scenarios: Identify coaching scenarios that are relevant to your work or organization. Conduct a practice between a "coach", "coachee" and "observer" that will allow each person to practice being a coach for each of the following elements of the coaching model:
   a. Goal
   b. Reality
   c. Obstacles/Options
   d. Way Forward

4. Observer: Pair up to practice giving feedback using the BICA model – Behavior, Impact, Consequences, Action.

5. Coaching Conversation: Use a tool to help you prepare for a coaching conversation that you need to have.

The following one-pager can be used as a tool for your upcoming coaching conversations. If you were not a participant in the workshop and are a little confused, that is okay! Continue using this workbook and you can be prepared to have your own coaching conversations and begin to impact the coaching culture in your organization.

Enhanced DNA: Develop Nurture Achieve, LLC

Coaching Conversation Worksheet

Use this worksheet to prepare for an individual coaching conversation. Ensure that this is not an "instruction", "feedback" or "discipline" conversation, and then proceed with the following preparation.

GROW Model of Coaching	
G – Goal	What are you trying to achieve? Define the goals and objectives.
R – Reality	What is happening now? Identify the current situation.
O – Obstacles/Options	What are the barriers? Identify what is keeping the employee from completing the goal. What options do you have? Brainstorm potential things that can be done.
W – Way Forward	What directions or actions can will be taken? Identify steps and milestones to solve the problem.

Date: _____

Coach _____   **Coachee** _____

GOAL:
REALITY:
OBSTACLES:
OPTIONS:
WAY FORWARD:

Section 2: Beyond the Workshop:

How Do Leaders Maintain a Coaching Culture?

Now that you have had your review, let's get started with the culture! Just having one leader become fluent in the art of coaching is not enough. It has to transcend into the entire organization and the culture has to shift! In Section 2, we will dive into the weeds and discuss the following:

- Creating the Culture
- Nurturing the Culture
- Realizing the Culture Change
- Maintaining the Culture Change

As you begin this section, ask yourself the following questions:

1. How do I know that I am committed to creating a change in the culture?

_____

_____

_____

2. What steps am I willing to take to nurture the culture?

_____

_____

_____

3. What are the benefits of maintaining a culture in my organization?

_____

_____

_____

Enhanced DNA: Develop Nurture Achieve, LLC

Chapter I: Creating the Culture

A coaching culture can only be realized if it is created, developed and nurtured by leaders. The culture of an organization is defined by the leader and must be maintained by that leader (and all leaders in the organization). It is a trickle down effect that can only be accepted and fulfilled within the organization when the leader embraces the culture, shares the culture and lives the culture. A coaching culture can only be maintained if the leader effectively coaches, teaches others to coach and measures the success of the transformation of the organization as a result of the coaching culture.

What do we mean by culture? The culture of any organization is the organization's expectations, experiences, philosophy, and values that hold it together, and is expressed in its self-image, inner workings, interactions with the outside world, and any future expectations. When it comes to a coaching culture, coaching has to become a part of the expectations and values of the organization such that it occurs without effort and with buy-in from all involved. It will be accomplished because, not only do the leaders want it, those across the organization also expect it and will even demand it!

Why do those in the organization demand it? Because the coaching culture provides the ability for growth and development. Growth of individuals leads to the growth of the organization. As leaders demonstrate that they value those in the organization and they are willing to help them strive for improvement, those in the organization will, in turn, respond by excelling and developing professionally (maybe even personally). Effective coaching has a far greater impact than just the improvements seen in the organization – it has the ability to change lives.

When leaders create a coaching culture, the organization transforms because those impacted know that the leadership has their best interest at heart, that they are valued and that they will succeed because of the environment of culture is authentic.

Are you ready to change the culture? Take this simple assessment.

On a scale of 1 – 10 where 1 is "I'm lost and not sure where to start" and 10 is "I'm ready and have the tools to impact the culture", rate yourself in these areas:

_____ I have established a purpose and assessed the risk if we do not transform to a coaching culture.

_____ I am ready to lead by example.

_____ I know how to ask the right questions.

_____ I have a learn/do attitude.

_____ I know that the culture change starts at the top.

_____ I understand the coaching process and can model it in my organization.

_____ I know how to gain "buy-in" for the coaching process.

_____ I am willing to commit the time and energy to provide training and tools to impact the culture in the organization

_____ I am prepared to hold leaders accountable to the culture change.

💡 Don't let a good idea get away!

_____

_____

_____

_____

_____

_____

_____

_____

Chapter II: Nurturing the Culture

A coaching culture will result in a transformation of the organization to a growth mindset. In an organization that has been stagnant where coaching has not been effective, once the leadership demonstrates the desire to coach and develop those within the organization, it will be obvious within the organization and they will begin to respond. But that doesn't happen on its own.

Complete the following template to ensure that you can verbalize why the culture change is important. What is the impact of culture change to the people, the desired results and to relationships? As the leader, you should be able to verbalize this, so here is your guide to develop those messages.

Why Coach? Verbalizing your "Why":

Impact to the Organization	My Why
People	
Results	
Relationships	
Others?	

Now, let's start at the beginning. The leader will need to communicate the desire and expectations around the change in culture. A new vision or new mission will need to be developed along with the expectations of other leaders within the organization. A plan will need to be developed (because a change in culture cannot come automatically) and steps will need to be identified to implement against the plan and measure success against the plan.

Considerations for an Effective Plan

Identify the desired change (goal): Use SMAART goals – see Chapter 3.
Identify the desired outcomes:
Identify a communication plan:
Identify success measures:
Identify a timeline:
Evaluate the results:
REPEAT

Leaders who effectively coach and create a coaching culture will pave the way for a myriad of benefits within the organization but most of all, the culture change will be the foundation for meaningful connections and positive working relationships for all.

Enhanced DNA: Develop Nurture Achieve, LLC

Chapter III: Realizing the Culture Change

In order for the culture to shift, the leader will provide direction and guidance to all leaders in the organization and that direction and guidance will need to trickle down throughout the organization. But it first starts with the leaders demonstrating the coaching behaviors to their direct reports. This involves teaching (by example) what the expectations are related to coaching. It may need to start with education so that everyone is on the same page – with terminology and especially with a process. Coaching is not just a random action; it requires thought and preparation to be effective.

To realize the shift, it takes time and patience in establishing coaching excellence. It is important to recognize positive examples when they occur and leverage coaching as a strength throughout the entire organization. Once the shift begins to occur, those impacted will realize that the culture change is all about them – it provides development and growth throughout the entire organization. Think about this equation:

WHAT + HOW = Increase in Productivity, Results and Employee Engagement

In order to impact productivity, results and employee engagement in a positive way, use COACHING (as the what) and the CULTURE CHANGE (as the how). It is important to effectively know how to change the culture and we will do that through the Coaching Model – GROW.

Enhanced DNA: Develop Nurture Achieve, LLC

The Model:

We support any defined coaching process; however, we will focus on the GROW Model of Coaching since it is a simple methodology that can be replicated in any organization or environment that is willing to put some effort and energy in each step.

GROW Model of Coaching*	
G - Goal	What are you trying to achieve? Define the goals and objectives.
R - Reality	What is happening now? Identify the current situation.
O – Obstacles/Options	What are the barriers? Identify what is keeping the employee from completing the goal. What options do you have? Brainstorm potential things that can be done.
W – Way Forward	What directions or actions can will be taken? Identify steps and milestones to solve the problem.

*There have been many claims to authorship of the GROW model as a way of achieving goals and solving problems. While no one person can be clearly identified as the originator, Graham Alexander, Alan Fine, and Sir John Whitmore all made significant contributions.

I. GOAL: Setting Goals

The first step in the GROW Coaching Model is defining the goal for each person that you plan to coach (the coachee). We will also introduce another methodology to assist with setting goals and that is the SMART process. We like to incorporate an extra A into the process: SMAART Goals.

SMAART goals should be:

S - Specific
M - Measurable
A – Attainable
A – Accountable
R- Realistic
T – Timely

1.   SPECIFIC: In order for a goal to be effectively met, it must be specific – clearly defined and narrowed down to a point where it is able to be accomplished. To set specific goals, you can answer the following questions:

*Who: Who is involved?
*What: What do I want to accomplish?
*When: Establish a time frame.
*Where: Identify a location.
*Why: Specific reasons, purpose or benefits of accomplishing the goal.

2.   MEASURABLE: You must be able to put metrics around your goals – make it quantifiable so that the goal doesn't get lost. I prefer to "chunk" my goals into smaller pieces with shorter timelines and measurements. When you measure your progress, you stay on track, reach your target dates, and experience "intermittent reinforcement" of the ability to reach a goal.
To determine if your goal is measurable, ask questions such as……

·   By when?

Enhanced DNA: Develop Nurture Achieve, LLC

- How much?
- How many?
- How will I know when it is accomplished?

3.   ATTAINABLE: It is very important to set goals and measurements that are attainable – able to be achieved. If you set unrealistic goals, you will get discouraged and drop the goal. You can attain most any goal you set when you make a plan and establish a realistic timeframe that allows you to carry out those steps. Goals that may have seemed far away and out of reach eventually move closer and become more attainable, not because your goals shrink, but because you grow and expand to match them.

4.   REALISTIC: To be realistic, you have to have a sensible and practical idea of what can be achieved or expected. You have to be willing and able to get the work done. You have to be true to yourself about what you are willing to do to accomplish that goal – you are the only one who can determine how much or how high your goal should be.

5.   TIMELY: Your goals should be time bound. With no timeframe associated with your goals, you may not have the sense of urgency to complete the goal and you may never complete the goal – it becomes an ongoing project. If you continue to miss the timeframe set, reevaluate the goal to make sure that you "chunked" it appropriately. Break it down and reset your expectations.

6.   You may have noticed that there is an extra "A" in this acronym and it stands for ACCOUNTABLE: None of the other steps matter if you don't hold yourself accountable! Doing what is required and expected to complete your goals is only important if you recognize the successes and the failures. If your goals are met, celebrate them and if they are not met, call yourself out and regroup! Identify barriers to completing the goal and map out a new plan – chunking the goals, identifying new goals, different metrics or even changing the timeframe if needed.

Sample Goal Questions:
What would you like to accomplish?
What are your goals?
What is one goal you would like to focus on?
How does this goal fit into the big picture?
What does success look like?
What timeframe or what milestones would you have for this goal?
How will you know that you have reached or accomplished your goal?
How will you measure success?

Identify specific Goal questions that can be used for each person that you plan to coach.

Goal Questions:

After you have agreed upon the goal with your coachee, then ask whether the goal is a SMAART goal. Continue to review the goal with them until all aspects of SMAART are fulfilled.

II. REALITY: What is the current situation?

   Step 2 in the GROW Coaching Model is becoming aware of the current situation. This involves some self-evaluation to determine the follow-up. You cannot identify Obstacles, Options or the Way Forward until you realistically identify where you are right now.

   When a leader facilitates a coachee through the REALITY step, it is important to identify any patterns or themes that would keep the coachee from moving forward in the process. For example: Does the coachee have multiple projects that will keep them from focusing on the current situation? This may be addressed as an obstacle but it has to be identified as a current status before moving on.

Sample Reality Questions:
How are things going right now?
What barriers or conflicts do you have that will keep you from accomplishing this goal?
What are your priorities?
What resources do you have to accomplish your goal?
What is going well?
What have you done so far?
What are examples of issues you are facing?
What else do you need to accomplish this goal?

Identify specific Reality questions that can be used for each person that you plan to coach.

Reality Questions:

Once the leader is comfortable with the current status, then they can begin to identify any obstacles and seek options.

Enhanced DNA: Develop Nurture Achieve, LLC

III. OBSTACLES/OPTIONS:

Step III has two parts: Identifying obstacles and what are the options. We will break this into separate sections.

OBSTACLES: Identifying Barriers

There could be obstacles that are stopping the coachee from getting where they are, to accomplishing their goal. If there are no obstacles, the coachee should be ready to move to options, however, they will need to agree that there are no obstacles but if some arise, they must be addressed.

Sample Obstacle Questions:
What obstacles are keeping you from meeting this goal?
Why is this an obstacle?
If this obstacle is not removed, what is the impact?
Are there any other barriers?
What barriers could pop up that will impact this project?
If a barrier is not addressed, how can this delay or impact the project?

Identify specific Obstacle questions that can be used for each person that you plan to coach.

Obstacle Questions:

Once the leader is comfortable with the obstacles, then they can begin to identify Options.

Enhanced DNA: Develop Nurture Achieve, LLC

OPTIONS: Generating Ideas

Generating ideas that can contribute ideas for the solution to the problem (or goal) is important. As a coach, it is important that you allow the coachee the opportunity to brainstorm those options. In fact, the key role of the coach is to make sure that this is an interactive process where the coachee identifies the options and the coach probes (or asks questions) related to those ideas. For example: If the coachee brainstorms an idea that the coach may not be able to support, the first question from the coach might be "WHY?". Probe to get to an understanding of the idea/option and if it still does not align with what you believe the best path forward should be, continue asking the "WHY" question until the coachee realizes a different option or convinces you that it is an appropriate option to pursue.

In addition to facilitating the idea generation process, the coach should encourage a creative brainstorming process without conditionality – in order to generate a list of options and then structure those options to actions. Only in a situation where there is total brain-lock, should be coach add suggestions into the option gathering process. The coachee will be much more engaged in completing the goal when they have had the most input to the goal and the options for the solution. It gives them a sense of ownership to the goal and completing it.

Enhanced DNA: Develop Nurture Achieve, LLC

Sample Options Questions:

What would you do if you had no obstacles?

What other ways could this be accomplished?

If barriers were removed what could you do?

What is the advantage/disadvantage of that option?

What order of priority would you give each option?

What criteria will you use to evaluate that option?

Identify specific Options questions that can be used for each person that you plan to coach.

Options Questions:

Once the leader is comfortable with the options, then they can begin to identify the Way Forward.

IV. WAY FORWARD:

The final step of the GROW Coaching Model is mapping out the Way Forward. This will be a concrete plan of action. Once this is formalized, then the coachee will have the maximum opportunity for success with their goal.

Sample Way Forward Questions:
Which options can most effectively help you reach your goal?
How committed are you to this plan?
What options will you use and what is the priority of the options you selected?
What are some concrete steps that you can take now to move you forward?
What is the order of steps that you plan to take?
What support do you need to move forward with this plan?
Will this plan get you to your goal?
How can I help you accomplish this goal?

Enhanced DNA: Develop Nurture Achieve, LLC

Identify specific Way Forward questions that can be used for each person that you plan to coach.

Way Forward Questions:

Once the leader is comfortable with the Way Forward, then the coachee can begin the work.

Enhanced DNA: Develop Nurture Achieve, LLC

Chapter IV: Maintaining the Culture

You may realize that this is just the framework for making a culture shift and transforming the organization. In order for leaders to continue to make a difference, they need a few more skills. Effective leaders gain credibility and trust by demonstrating strong communication skills consistently.

1. Listening:

Effective leaders recognize the value of listening in their conversations and especially with coaching. They characterize their commitment to the organization and to the people in the organization. Effective leaders don't just passively listen; they actively listen and seek information others may miss.

Some key steps to active listening:

- Be Self-Aware – Effective leaders need to be aware of their strengths and be aware of any blind spots they may have. This is especially important in the ability to actively listen. Leaders should ensure that they are asking for feedback and acting upon any feedback. If people in the organization are not willing to participate in the coaching process, it could be that the leader is not a good listener and may not be appropriately engaging in the coaching process.

- Put others first - Put others first and inspire others by allowing them to speak and share ideas rather than providing the answers. Effective leaders listen for what motivates employees and provides benefits. They build their subsequent messages to meet the needs of others. and can read between the lines to find what inspires someone's thought processes and perspectives.

- Model the behavior - Effective leaders who are successful in their daily interactions are consistent in their listening skills each and every day. They are committed to demonstrating their listening skills, no matter the importance of the conversation. Effective leaders understand that their ability to listen is as critical to their impact on others as their ability to communicate. They recognize the importance of setting positive examples and modeling the kinds of skills they want employees to adopt.

2. Connecting:

There is more to communication that just talking. It is important that leaders actually "connect" with those in the organization in order to influence others to succeed. What does this mean? It means that leaders go beyond communication to making a connection with others.

Skills to be a connector:

- Connecting is all about others and not ourselves. People want to know that the leader cares for them, that they can help them and that they can trust them.
- Connecting goes beyond words. It is not just what the leader says, it is also about what people see, what they hear, what they feel as a result of what the leader does and the behaviors they exhibit.
- Connecting requires effort. It takes a lot of energy to connect. Connecting requires that the leader take initiative, be clear in their expectations, demonstrate patience and they should connect because they want to and not because it is the right thing to do.
- Connecting is a skill all in itself. Anyone can learn how to make every interaction an opportunity for a connection. But it will take practice. It involves demonstrating your own confidence, authenticity, credibility and your ability to be trusted.

3. The Trust Factor:

Trust is all about being trustworthy, assured reliance on the character, ability and strength of confidence place in someone. An effective leader must demonstrate trust and be trustworthy in all situations. They must exhibit all of the following in order to earn and maintain trust.

- Character – the leader must honor commitments and keep promises; ensure that private and public actions match
- Care – the leader must demonstrate empathy with others and create a safe environment for open conversations
- Competence – the leader must leverage their strengths and demonstrate fairness in decision-making

4. Build Accountability into the Culture:

Are you behaving like you want others to behave? Are you asking the right questions? Are you rating performance based off how well your leaders are coaching others? If you see that people are not being impacted, that results are not improving or that relationships are not improving, then coaching may not be occurring and you may need to address the gaps.

5. Lead By Example:

This is called the "domino effect". If the leader is not modeling the behavior, then those around them will not make the culture change.

6. Keep Coaching Consistent and Simple:

The GROW model of coaching is a simple method to use and can easily be remembered in any setting. Use this model consistently and it will become second nature.

Coaching culture delivers a great promise – a high-performance environment that holds people accountable for delivering results, while fostering a climate of full engagement, personal development and mutual respect – especially between the coach and the coachee.

Chapter 5: What Happens When Coaching Doesn't Work?

Coaching works for those willing to be coached, has an open mind and a strong desire to improve. So, what do you do when they don't want to be coached? When someone is resistant to coaching, their behaviors or attitudes do not align to the coaching process or their habits demonstrate that they are not on board, you have to take action to address those behaviors, attitudes or habits.

Remember that there are times when coaching is not the right answer.

1. When giving instructions to complete and assignment or project – education or training.
2. When addressing a performance issue – feedback to address behaviors or skill gaps.
3. When delivering discipline.

Education or training:

Situations that involve a technical subject, training or functional skill development do not require coaching unless you are working together to solve a problem that the person already has the skills to perform. If not, this is a learning opportunity. Once the skills are achieved and the person is ready to perform those skills, then you can move to a coaching situation.

Resistance:

The first step to dealing with someone who is resistant to coaching is to understand why they are resistant. Could there be a logical, reasonable explanation as to why they don't want to engage in coaching? As the leader, you need to recognize that the person is resistant. They could be passive in the discussion, avoiding the entire conversation or doesn't respond to the plans put in place. This requires a "crucial conversation" to help you understand what barriers exist and why they are resistant. In this situation, you need to pause the coaching conversation to address the resistance. As you prepare for this conversation, make sure that you are willing to listen to help troubleshoot and put actions in place. Here are some potential reasons they could be resistant:

Enhanced DNA: Develop Nurture Achieve, LLC

- Trust – Is there a trust issue between you and the person you are attempting to coach? Are they unsure of the "motive" for the coaching conversation?
- Appreciation – Do they understand the value and benefit of the coaching process? You may need to revisit the "Why Coaching?" conversation.
- Knowledge – There could be a gap in the knowledge of the subject you are trying to coach on – they just don't know. This will be evident as you ask your coaching questions and the answer is "I don't know". They really may not know. This takes you back to the education/training piece and you may need to re-train or re-educate. If this is a topic that is a key requirement of their job responsibilities, you may also need to address that from a performance perspective – not coaching.

Discipline:

Once you address the skill gaps through education and training, if the person is not improving in performance and is unable to engage in a coaching conversation on that topic, you should consider implementing your company discipline processes. At minimum, you should ensure that you are providing the feedback, identifying the gaps and put a performance improvement plan in place to address the issues.

The key is not to "force" coaching – make sure that coaching is the appropriate tool.

 Don't let a good idea get away!

_____

_____

_____

_____

_____

_____

_____

Enhanced DNA: Develop Nurture Achieve, LLC

Chapter 6: Beyond the Workshop - Tools

This is just the beginning. Through this workbook, we have provided tools for a successful implementation. You can also use the following action guide to ensure that you take practical steps to transform your organization through Coaching for Success.

Using the chart below, identify specific actions that you can either apply right away, change over time or teach to others. Write those actions in the left column. Identify options of actions that you can take either apply, change or teach related to that topic. Once you have several action items, prioritize in order to put your plan in place.

Coaching for Success

	APPLY	CHANGE	TEACH

You Can Achieve a Coaching Culture!

Enhanced DNA: Develop Nurture Achieve, LLC

Section 3: Additional Coaching Questions to Consider

GOAL QUESTIONS:

- What do you really want?
- What is your short term goal? What is your long term goal?
- What is your vision?
- What is your next evolutionary step?
- Where do you want to be in 1 year? 5 years? 10 years?
- What is your motivation for achieving this goal?
- Does this goal align to your beliefs/values?
- What is your most important project?
- What are some immediate steps you can take to achieve your goals?
- What can you do that will make you feel like you have a win/win situation?
-
-
-
-
-

Enhanced DNA: Develop Nurture Achieve, LLC

REALITY QUESTIONS:

- What is the biggest challenge you have?
- What are you putting up with?
- What has worked well? What has not worked well?
- What is your current strategy to achieve your goal?
- What are you giving up to achieve your goals?
- What successes have you had?
- What is your role in any issue?
- How long have you been working toward this goal?
- What is getting in your way to achieving success?
- What is your biggest fear to succeeding?
-
-
-
-
-

OBSTACLES QUESTIONS:

- What changes should you make to meet your goal?
- How much freedom is your reality causing?
- How will you know if you are overextending yourself?
- What are you tolerating?
- What are you sacrificing to accomplish your goal?
- How will you know if you should discontinue your efforts?
- What conflicts are you having?
- What support do you need?
- What are you wasting your time with?
- What can you delegate?
-
-
-
-
-

Enhanced DNA: Develop Nurture Achieve, LLC

OPTIONS QUESTIONS:

- Who else can help you with this project?
- How can I help?
- What can you do differently?
- What do you need to know that you don't know?
- How do your values impact solutions?
- What can you do today to get you on track?
- What could happen to change your mind?
- How might you break that down into steps?
- What do you need to know that you don't already know?
- What technology would improve your chances for success?
-
-
-
-
-

Enhanced DNA: Develop Nurture Achieve, LLC

WAY FORWARD QUESTIONS:

- Have you weighed all options?
- Have you addressed all obstacles?
- How "perfect" is your plan?
- How are you feeling about your direction?
- Are you ready to begin?
- Before you begin, are there any changes that you would make?
- Have you identified all milestones?
- What will success look like?
- If everything went the way you planned, what would be the best possible outcome?
- What do you need from me?
-
-
-
-
-

Enhanced DNA: Develop Nurture Achieve, LLC

Thank you for committing to a Coaching Culture in your organization. For bulk copies of this workbook, or for a FREE consultation to discuss workshops and Leadership training to transform and impact the culture within your organization, please contact us:

https://developnurtureachieve.com/contact.

Enhanced DNA: Develop Nurture Achieve, LLC

ABOUT THE AUTHOR

Denola M. Burton is the Founder and CEO of Enhanced DNA: Develop Nurture Achieve, LLC. She is a natural nurturer and brings over 20 years of Human Resources experience and expertise to challenge everyone to grow and develop wherever they are in their life or careers.

Denola holds a Bachelor and Master of Science degrees in Biology. After beginning her career as a scientist, she transitioned into Human Resources in 1996 where she began to live her passion! Denola is certified as a Professional in Human Resources from both the Society for Human Resource Management (SHRM-CP), and the Human Resource Certification Institute (HRCI-PHR). She is a Certified DISC Behavioral Coach through Institute Success and is a Certified Speaker, Trainer, Coach with the John Maxwell Team.

Through Enhanced DNA: Develop Nurture Achieve, Denola is poised and equipped to develop and nurture individuals and organizations to enhance their Leadership, Communication and Performance DNA. Denola is the author of her first book, a memoir, If You Really Knew Me: The Life, The Lessons and The Legacy, and as a result of the lessons learned during the publishing process, she became a member of the Independent Book Publishing Association and created the Enhanced DNA Publishing Division of her company.

Denola retired in December, 2017 from Eli Lilly and Company, a Fortune 500 pharmaceutical company where her career spanned over 27 years. She has been married to her husband, Phillip, for over 26 years and they have two daughters, Danielle and

Ciara. Denola focuses on living a life of "significance" by adding value through her business endeavors and through her family and friends.

Books by Denola M. Burton

- If You Really Knew Me: The Life, The Lessons and The Legacy
- Enhancing Your Leadership DNA: Coaching For Success
- Enhancing Your Communication DNA: Publishing For Beginners
- Enhancing Your Performance DNA: Mentoring For Success
- Mentoring Moments: 14 Remarkable Women Share Breakthroughs to Success
- Mentoring Moments: Journal to Success

All Available at www.EnhancedDNAPublishingon Amazon

Connect with me:

Email	DenolaBurton@EnhancedDNA1.com
Website	www.DevelopNurtureAchieve.com
	www.EnhancedDNAPublishing.com
Facebook	Enhanced DNA Develop Nurture Achieve
	Enhanced DNA Publishing
Instagram	@Enhanced_DNA
Twitter	@EnhancedDNA

Enhanced DNA: Develop Nurture Achieve, LLC

Denola M. Burton, CEO and Founder

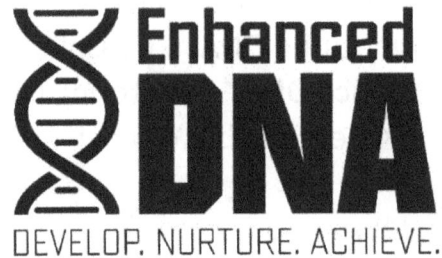

Workshop Options:

Enhancing Your Leadership DNA

- Coaching for Success

Enhancing Your Communication DNA

- Everyone Communicates, Few Connect
- Publishing for Beginners

Enhancing Your Performance DNA

- Mentoring for Success

- Bringing Behaviors and Performance to Life Through DISC

For more information: https://developnurtureachieve.com/contact

on: https://developnurtureachieve.com/contact

www.ingramcontent.com/pod-product-compliance
Lightning Source LLC
Chambersburg PA
CBHW081652270326
41933CB00018B/3440